THIS CANDLEWICK BOOK BELONGS TO:

_____

_____

_____

Step Gently Out

poem by
Helen Frost

photographs by
Rick Lieder

CANDLEWICK PRESS

Step gently out,

be still,
and watch
a single blade
of grass.

An ant
climbs up
to look
around.

A honeybee flies past.

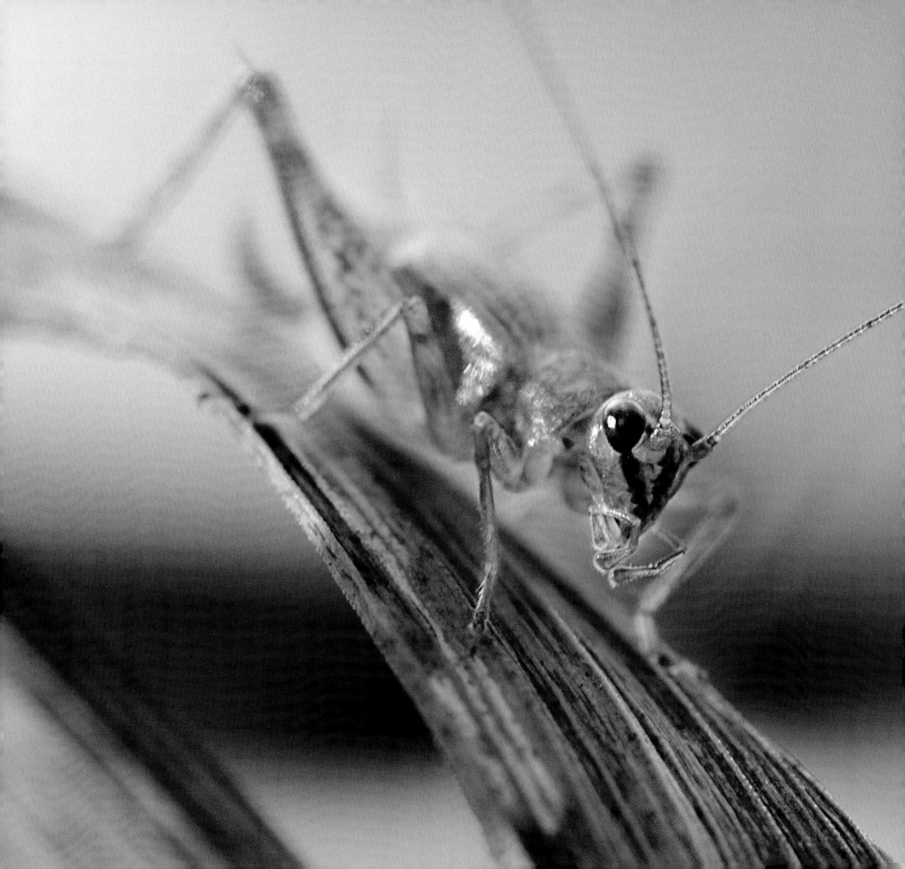

A cricket leaps
and lands,
then sits back
and sings.

A moth flies
in and comes
to rest with
open wings.

A spider
spins a silken thread
and steps
across
the
air.

A praying mantis
looks at you—

Balanced lightly
on a leaf,

bathed in golden light,

flashing,
Look,
I'm over here,

as evening

turns to

night,

the
creatures
shine with
stardust,

they're
splashed
with
morning
dew.

In song and dance
and stillness,

they share the world
with you.

European Honeybee

You may see honeybees flying from flower to flower, gathering nectar and pollen to take back to their hives. In each hive, a large colony of honeybees lives together. The colony has one queen bee, several hundred drones, and thousands of worker bees. The worker bees use nectar to make honey to feed the young. They also make wax to build the walls of the hive.

Chinese Praying Mantis

Adult praying mantises are large insects that live in fields and gardens. They are often well camouflaged, making them hard to see. They can be very still while they wait for their prey, turning their head from side to side without moving their legs and wings. When their prey comes near, they move fast, catching and holding the prey while they eat it.

Tussock Moth Caterpillar

Caterpillars are one stage in the life cycle of butterflies and moths. After hatching, they spend their life eating and growing bigger. Then they form a cocoon or chrysalis, from which the moth or butterfly will emerge. Caterpillars are often colorful and can be very beautiful, but if they have tufts of hair, don't touch them — they can sting or give you a rash.

Eastern Black Carpenter Ant *(top)*
Pavement Ant *(bottom)*

Ants are found almost everywhere in the world. They live in colonies in which different ants have different jobs. They are most active in warm weather. Ants spend much of their time in underground tunnels, but you can see them climbing on grass and trees and flowers as they look for food.

Big Dipper Firefly

Fireflies are beetles that can light up in the dark. They use their lights to flash signals to one another, sending different signals by the length and timing of their flashes. They are most active at night, flying, then stopping to rest in the grass or on bushes and trees. They like damp places, so if you go out to look for them, look near water or go out after it has rained.

Greater Angle-wing Katydid

Katydids are usually green or brown, but they can also be other colors — even bright pink. They often live near the tops of trees, camouflaged by their leaf-like wings. You might see them on the ground or climbing up a tree trunk. The males and females call to one another by making a sound something like their name: *katydid, katydid, katydid.*

Ebony Jewelwing Damselfly

Look for damselflies near streams and ponds, flying just above the water or resting on rocks and plants. They often have brightly colored bodies and lacy wings. While they are flying, you may see them catch and eat other insects. When they stop to rest, they usually fold their wings over their bodies.

Striped Ground Cricket

Although they have wings, crickets are more likely to jump than fly. Some crickets can jump three feet in the air. You will probably hear a cricket before you see one. Male crickets make a chirping sound by rubbing one wing against the other. Listen for crickets on summer evenings. And look for them in the grass, on bushes, or under stones.

Chickweed Geometer Moth

Moths, like butterflies, have four wings covered with tiny scales which give them their color patterns. Most moths have feathery antennae. Moths are usually more active at night, but the moth in this book often flies during the day. Look for it in fields and meadows, lawns and gardens, flying from plant to plant or resting with its wings held out flat.

Orb-weaver Spider

Spiders are often found around the edges of houses, under rocks, near drainpipes, on bushes, or in the grass. Some spiders spin webs that stretch from one branch to another. Early on a summer morning, when light shines on drops of dew that have formed on a spiderweb, the web is easier to see. When you see a web, you will often find a spider.

Common Yellow Jacket

Yellow jackets are a type of wasp; they are about half an inch long, with large black eyes and a definite "waist." They live in colonies in which different wasps have different jobs. Except for the queen, the rest of the colony dies off in the winter. You may see them flying in and out of their nest or looking for sweet food and drinks. The females can sting, so don't get too close.

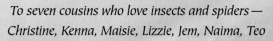

To seven cousins who love insects and spiders —
Christine, Kenna, Maisie, Lizzie, Jem, Naima, Teo

H. F.

For Kathe,
and a backyard full of small friends

R. L.

Text copyright © 2012 by Helen Frost. Photographs copyright © 2012 by Rick Lieder. All rights reserved. No part of this book may be reproduced, transmitted, or stored in an information retrieval system in any form or by any means, graphic, electronic, or mechanical, including photocopying, taping, and recording, without prior written permission from the publisher. First paperback edition 2018. Library of Congress Cataloging-in-Publication Data is available. Library of Congress Catalog Card Number 2015298697. ISBN 978-0-7636-5601-0 (hardcover), ISBN 978-0-7636-9517-0 (paperback). This book was typeset in Tiepolo. Candlewick Press, 99 Dover Street, Somerville, Massachusetts 02144. visit us at www.candlewick.com. Printed in Humen, Dongguan, China.   22 APS 10 9 8 7 6

Helen Frost is the author of *Sweep Up the Sun, Among a Thousand Fireflies*, and *Wake Up!*, as well as several other award-winning books for children and young adults. About *Step Gently Out*, she says, "When I first saw Rick's photographs, they reminded me of being a child and watching insects for hours. So I went outdoors and looked closely and I discovered that the insects were still there, all around me." Helen Frost lives in Fort Wayne, Indiana.

Rick Lieder is a photographer, painter, and illustrator. He is the photographer of *Sweep Up the Sun, Among a Thousand Fireflies*, and *Wake Up!* About *Step Gently Out*, he says, "Often the smallest creatures around us are the most amazing." Rick Lieder lives in Michigan.